Sports Innovations

INNOVATIONS IN BASKETBALL

by Chris Sheridan

SportsZone

An Imprint of Abdo Publishing
abdobooks.com

abdobooks.com

Published by Abdo Publishing, a division of ABDO, PO Box 398166, Minneapolis, Minnesota 55439. Copyright © 2022 by Abdo Consulting Group, Inc. International copyrights reserved in all countries. No part of this book may be reproduced in any form without written permission from the publisher. SportsZone™ is a trademark and logo of Abdo Publishing.

Printed in the United States of America, North Mankato, Minnesota.
102021
012022

Cover Photos: Eric Christian Smith/AP Images, left; AP Images, right
Interior Photos: AP Images, 5, 7, 13; Patrick Semansky/AP Images, 8; Richard Carson/AP Images, 10; Bettmann/Getty Images, 14; Focus on Sport/Getty Images, 17, 18; Paul Vathis/AP Images, 21; Nick Ut/AP Images, 23; Matt Strasen/AP Images, 25; J.M. Hogan/AP Images, 27; Brian Rothmuller/Icon Sportswire/AP Images, 29; Lennox McLendon/AP Images, 31; Mark Duncan/AP Images, 33; Jeff Chiu/AP Images, 35; Susan Ragan/AP Images, 37; Charlie Riedel/AP Images, 39; Don Ryan/AP Images, 41; Matt Slocum/AP Images, 43

Editor: Katie Chanez
Series Designer: Joshua Olson

Library of Congress Control Number: 2020949105

Publisher's Cataloging-in-Publication Data

Names: Sheridan, Chris, author.
Title: Innovations in basketball / by Chris Sheridan
Description: Minneapolis, Minnesota : Abdo Publishing, 2022 | Series: Sports innovations | Includes online resources and index.
Identifiers: ISBN 9781532195037 (lib. bdg.) | ISBN 9781098215347 (ebook)
Subjects: LCSH: Basketball--Juvenile literature. | Technological innovations--Juvenile literature. | Sports sciences--Juvenile literature. | Performance technology--Juvenile literature. | Basketball--Equipment and supplies--Juvenile literature. | Sports--Juvenile literature.
Classification: DDC 688.76--dc23

TABLE OF CONTENTS

CHAPTER 1
TAKE A SHOT.................................... 4

CHAPTER 2
COLORFUL REVOLUTION 12

CHAPTER 3
BIG TO SMALL................................. 20

CHAPTER 4
CHUCK TAYLOR TO AIR JORDAN 26

CHAPTER 5
A LEAGUE OF STARS........................ 30

CHAPTER 6
THE WORLD OF BASKETBALL.............. 36

TIMELINE   44
HONORABLE MENTIONS   45
GLOSSARY   46
MORE INFORMATION   47
ONLINE RESOURCES   47
INDEX   48
ABOUT THE AUTHOR   48

CHAPTER 1

TAKE A SHOT

Basketball is one of the fastest, most dynamic games in the world. When it's played well, it seems the players are always on the run, the ball is moving all over the court, and the scoreboard is lit up like a pinball machine.

But that wasn't always the case. The National Basketball Association (NBA) was formed in 1949. And in its early days, the game looked a lot different from its modern form. One big difference is that a team with a talented big man could dominate the league. Few teams had a player who could match up with George Mikan of the Minneapolis Lakers. As a result, the 6-foot-10-inch center led the Lakers to five championships in six years.

In the 1949–50 season, Mikan scored a league-high 27.4 points per game. He began the next year on a tear as well, averaging 27.9 points over his first 10 games. That included

George Mikan, *right*, was one of the NBA's first superstars.

NEW YORK
8
NEW
LAKERS
99

a 47-point game as the Lakers beat the Rochester Royals on November 18, 1950.

STALL TACTICS

Four nights later, the Fort Wayne Pistons visited Minneapolis, where the Lakers had won 29 straight games. The Pistons didn't have a big man who could handle Mikan. And they didn't have the overall talent to keep up with the rest of the Lakers. So Fort Wayne coach Murray Mendenhall came up with a unique strategy. He figured, if you couldn't stop Mikan, you could at least slow him down.

And that's just what the Pistons did. They spent the game playing keep-away. Fort Wayne players held the ball and waited for the Lakers to come out and defend against them. Taken out of their game, the Lakers were rattled. The fans booed loudly. And in the end, the strategy worked. Fort Wayne scored a basket in the final 10 seconds to win the game 19–18.

After the game, Lakers coach John Kundla was irate. "Play like that will kill professional basketball," he fumed. And he wasn't the only one. NBA President Maurice Podoloff gathered team owners and other officials for a meeting in New York. Numerous proposals were made to ban stall tactics, but nothing was officially resolved. The teams made an

Maurice Podoloff served as the NBA president from the beginning of the league until 1963.

informal agreement to avoid such strategy in the future. But it took four more years to institute one of the game's most important innovations.

GET MOVING

At the NBA league meeting in April 1954, Syracuse Nationals owner Danny Biasone proposed that the league begin using a

While the NBA shot clock remains at 24 seconds, college basketball and other leagues experiment with different lengths of time.

24-second shot clock to speed up games. Why 24 seconds? The games were 48 minutes long. In a high-scoring game, Biasone estimated each team took approximately 60 shots, or 120 total shots. So 48 minutes divided by 120 shots equals 24 seconds per shot.

Podoloff and league owners agreed to give the shot clock a try. In the first game of the new season that fall, the Royals defeated the Boston Celtics 98–95. Mission accomplished.

Today, it's hard to imagine the NBA without the shot clock. And its success in speeding up the game has continued. In the 2019–20 season, every NBA team averaged at least 102.9 points per game. The Milwaukee Bucks led the way at 118.7. Needless to say, no game has come close to a 19–18 final score in years.

ON CAMPUS

College basketball was not so quick to adapt to the shot clock. With the great talent disparity between small and large schools, officials feared smaller teams would get run off the floor with a shot clock driving the tempo.

Hall of Fame men's coach Dean Smith of the University of North Carolina had his team thoroughly master what was known as the four corners offense. Smith would spread four of his players far apart in the offensive zone, with a fifth player in

Dean Smith often employed the four corners offense in his coaching strategy. This led to many low-scoring games.

the middle. Then they would pass the ball from player to player without ever taking a shot.

The strategy was to hold onto the ball for as long as possible without shooting. Low final scores—such as Duke 21, North Carolina 20 in 1966—were a natural byproduct of the strategy. Coaches used the strategy against stronger teams, or in a hostile atmosphere against a crowd packed with rowdy, loud college students. Or they'd employ the four corners offense late in a game when they were protecting a lead.

Tactically, it was brilliant. But it wasn't much fun to watch. In 1985 the National Collegiate Athletic Association (NCAA) changed the rule and put in a 45-second clock as a compromise. That allowed teams to hold onto the ball for a long time but not indefinitely. The shot clock was reduced to 35 seconds in 1993 and then to 30 seconds in 2015.

SUPER STALL

One of the lowest-scoring games in men's college basketball history took place on December 15, 1973. At one point in the game at Tennessee, the Temple Owls held the ball for 11 minutes 38 seconds without taking a shot. Tennessee led 7–5 at halftime and won by a final score of 11–6.

CHAPTER 2

COLORFUL
REVOLUTION

Before the 1960s, professional sports leagues had gone through a period of relative stability. The National Hockey League (NHL) played with the same six teams from 1942 to 1967. The same 12 teams made up the National Football League (NFL) from 1953 to 1959. In Major League Baseball (MLB), some teams changed cities, but the same 16 franchises comprised the league from 1916 to 1960.

The NBA took a few years to settle in after it was founded in 1949. But after the Baltimore Bullets folded in 1954, the league consisted of the same eight franchises until 1961.

That lack of growth wasn't due to a lack of interest. Plenty of cities around the growing United States wanted big-league sports teams of their own. And investors were lined up to purchase teams to join the established leagues. But they

caption: The NBA had only eight teams throughout much of the 1950s.

LAKERS
12

continued to find the door closed because the existing owners were happy with the way things were.

Instead of giving up in frustration, those outsiders did the next best thing. They formed their own leagues to challenge the existing structures. And those rebels ended up doing more to change the face of professional sports than anyone could have imagined.

The NBA added the Chicago Packers in 1961. The team later moved to Washington, DC, and eventually became the Wizards.

Other American sports leagues such as the NFL and NHL responded by adding teams in new cities. The NHL for example doubled in size in 1967 from six to 12 teams. With no major rival league, the NBA was a bit slower to adapt.

Several NBA teams moved in the 1960s, such as the Minneapolis Lakers to Los Angeles. But the league was slow to embrace expansion. It added one team in 1961, then another in 1966. That brought the league up to 10 teams, but that pace was about to increase.

SHAKING IT UP

The next year, the American Basketball Association (ABA) arrived. The ABA brought pro basketball to cities that didn't have NBA teams. They included Louisville, Kentucky; Pittsburgh, Pennsylvania; Denver, Colorado; Minneapolis, Minnesota; Indianapolis, Indiana; and Houston, Texas. Other underserved markets soon joined in the fun, including St. Louis, Missouri; Norfolk, Virginia; and San Antonio, Texas.

In response, the NBA started an expansion of its own. From 1966 to 1974, the NBA doubled from nine to 18 teams. Expansion occurred all over the country, from San Diego, California, to Buffalo, New York. But while the NBA could bring new teams to new cities, the ABA was offering fans something different on the court.

In order to attract fans to the new league, the ABA encouraged a fun, up-tempo style of play. Flashy uniforms were the norm. And the league's red, white, and blue ball is probably its most memorable contribution to the sport.

The ABA also was one of the first leagues to use the three-point shot. That innovation opened the floor and created a contrast with NBA, which still emphasized getting the ball as close to the basket as possible for a layup or a dunk. The NBA eventually adopted the three-pointer in 1979.

THROWING IT DOWN

Aside from the three-point shot, one other ABA legacy carried over to the NBA—the slam dunk contest. This was an invention that the ABA came up with in 1976 to generate excitement around its All-Star Game. Julius "Dr. J." Erving won it by soaring from the free-throw line for one of the most memorable dunks in history. It took the NBA until 1984 to add a dunk contest to its All-Star festivities. Once the league did, though, the dunk contest quickly became one of the weekend's most popular events.

The ABA was famous for its bright red, white, and blue basketball.

High-flying Julius Erving began his professional career in the ABA.

The rival league also helped players acquire leverage in contract negotiations. NBA veterans threatened to jump to the ABA, and some of them did, including Hall of Fame guard Rick Barry. And players coming out of college who were drafted by both leagues could pit the two teams against each other to drive up their salary offers.

The ABA eventually ran into financial difficulties. A number of teams folded after not being able to pay their players. Finally, in 1976 the league merged with the NBA. Only six teams remained at the time. Two of them—the Kentucky Colonels and the Spirits of St. Louis—were disbanded. The Denver Nuggets, Indiana Pacers, New York Nets, and San Antonio Spurs joined the NBA starting in the 1976–77 season, and the ABA was history.

However, every now and then on a playground or at a gym, a red-white-and-blue basketball flies through the air from beyond the three-point line. The colorful memory of the ABA lives on.

CHAPTER 3

BIG TO SMALL

Wilt Chamberlain didn't even want to score 100 points in a game. He was worried about rubbing it in against the hapless New York Knicks on March 2, 1962. But Philadelphia Warriors coach Frank McGuire kept his star center in the game. There was little the Knicks could do to stop him.

Chamberlain already held the NBA's single-game scoring record. He set it earlier that season. He broke the record of 71 points by scoring 78 in a triple overtime game back in December. Chamberlain was in the middle of a revolutionary season. He averaged more than 50 points per game in 1961–62. In the NBA's first season in 1948–49, the average for an entire team was just 80 points per game.

At 7-foot-1 and 275 pounds, Chamberlain was a matchup nightmare. Teams couldn't compete with him physically. Against the Knicks that night, Chamberlain made 36 field goals

caption: Wilt Chamberlain celebrates his epic 100-point game.

100
PHIL

and hit 28 free throws. His last basket gave him an even 100 for the game.

Chamberlain's dominant play changed the way basketball was played. He also injected some star power into the league. In 1962, the NBA was not a big-time venture. The Warriors-Knicks game that day was played in Hershey, Pennsylvania, in front of just a few thousand fans. The game wasn't televised. Only a few writers and photographers were on hand to cover it. Superstars like Chamberlain helped make the NBA into the globally popular league it is today. But the game itself is far different today compared to how it was played in 1962.

SPLASHING THREES

American Basketball League (ABL) commissioner Abe Saperstein advocated for his league to adopt a three-point line for its inaugural 1961–62 season. His goal was simple. He wanted the gameplay in his new league to be as exciting as possible.

In the days before the three-point line was part of the NBA, teams often focused on getting the ball to a big man for a dunk.

"We must have a weapon," Saperstein said. "And this is ours."

The ABL only lasted a season and a half, but other leagues around the world tried the three-point line in the years to come. The NBA added it in 1979. An extra point on a shot meant coaches had to adjust their thinking. As three-pointers became common at all levels, players got better at them.

But the three was still rarely attempted by players. In 1992–93 NBA teams averaged 734 three-point attempts. The Phoenix Suns led the league with 1,095 attempts. Over the rest of the 1990s, coaches and players started to see that the risk of a three was worth it, considering the reward for a successful shot.

By the 2012–13 season, 1,095 three-pointers were the fewest of any team in the NBA. Three teams took more than 2,000. The king of the three was Stephen Curry of the Golden State Warriors. Curry set the mark for most threes in a season that year with 272. He broke his own record in 2015. Then he did it again in 2016, when he topped 400.

In the 2015–16 season, Curry attempted 886 threes. That was more than the average for an entire team just 23 years earlier. Curry was the face of a new and exciting NBA. Rather than a big player who could bruise his way to the hoop, he was a sweet shooter who was deadly accurate. And Curry was not alone. He was not even alone on the Warriors.

With Golden State, Curry played alongside Klay Thompson. Together, they were known as the "Splash Brothers" for how they would "splash" in three-pointers. Thompson made

Stephen Curry (30) has set several records for three-pointers.

an NBA-record 14 three-pointers in a 2019 game against
the Chicago Bulls—doing it before the third quarter had
even ended.

CHAPTER 4

CHUCK TAYLOR TO
AIR JORDAN

Hockey players wear skates. Baseball and football players wear cleats. Basketball players wear sneakers that anyone can buy. But that doesn't mean players take their footwear for granted. Players have signature shoes that give them the performance and comfort they need to perform at their best.

The first signature shoe belonged to Chuck Taylor. He was not an NBA star. Taylor's playing days ended in the early 1920s. But as a salesman for the Converse shoe company, he knew just what players wanted. Taylor helped design a new sneaker and traveled the country, putting on basketball clinics and promoting the new shoe.

Taylor was such a great salesman that the company named the shoe after him in 1934. His signature appears on the heel of every pair of Chuck Taylor All-Stars, which are still sold today.

caption: Many early basketball players wore Chuck Taylor All-Stars.

NBA players wore them well into the 1980s. Taylor himself was inducted into the Naismith Memorial Basketball Hall of Fame in 1968.

JORDAN TAKES FLIGHT

People were shocked when a rookie basketball player named Michael Jordan signed a shoe contract worth $2.5 million in 1984. Jordan hadn't even played an NBA game yet. And the shoe company Nike was more associated with track and field than hoops.

The shoe came out in 1985. A pair was priced at $65, a lot of money for shoes at the time. But by then Jordan was one of the most popular players in the NBA. His high-flying dunks earned him the nickname "Air Jordan," and that's what the shoes were called.

Jordan's shoes were the colors of his Chicago Bulls, red and black. The NBA at the time had rules about colored sneakers and fined Jordan $5,000 per game. Nike paid the fine to keep Jordan's popular shoes on

AIR SWOOPES

NBA superstars had long had signature shoes by the time Sheryl Swoopes became the first woman to get one. Swoopes was a star for Team USA and got her shoe in 1995 in advance of the 1996 Olympic Games. The Air Swoopes from Nike featured a low cut on the ankle so Swoopes could make her quick moves on the court.

Air Jordan shoes are still popular and collectable, both on and off the court.

the court. Today, the Air Jordan brand is still going strong. And it was the first of many signature shoes NBA players have had.

But basketball shoes are about more than just looking good. Basketball players' feet and ankles take a pounding over the course of a game. The comfort and durability of the shoe is what's most important. Today's shoes are lighter and tougher than ever.

A LEAGUE OF
STARS

For fans of NBA history, it is easy to picture the all-time greats and the teams for which they played. Larry Bird wore a Boston Celtics uniform. Magic Johnson spent his career in the purple and gold of the Los Angeles Lakers. Isiah Thomas was a Detroit Piston.

But what about superstar LeBron James? Will fans remember him as a Cleveland Cavalier, where he played most of his seasons? Or as a member of the Miami Heat, where he won two titles? Or will they remember his time with the Lakers, one of the NBA's most popular teams?

In today's NBA, star players change teams more often than they did in the 1970s and 1980s. The NBA today is often referred to as a players' league. One player can have a lot of

caption:

Many former NBA superstars, such as Magic Johnson, *left*, and Larry Bird, *right*, spent the majority of their careers with the same teams.

power in a sport that only has a dozen or so guys per team. The NBA's superstars are who people come to see.

THE DECISION

In the summer of 2010, LeBron James had a decision to make. His contract with the Cavaliers was up, and he was a free agent for the first time. James was the best player in the NBA. The world eagerly awaited his choice. Would he stay home in Ohio or go to one of the NBA's bigger markets?

James's announcement was televised in a one-hour show on ESPN. It was called *The Decision*, and it aired on July 8, 2010. Ten million people tuned in just to see James speak. He changed the NBA with one simple sentence.

"I'm going to take my talents to South Beach and join the Miami Heat," James said.

Heat fans celebrated. Fans of other hopeful teams despaired. Cavaliers owner Dan Gilbert called the decision an act of "cowardly betrayal."

Fans criticized James because Miami wasn't only signing him. The Heat had also re-signed Dwyane Wade and lured free agent Chris Bosh away from Toronto. Both players were All-Stars, and Miami was considered a "superteam."

Cleveland fans were outraged when LeBron James announced his decision to move to Miami.

People thought that James was taking the easy route to a title with the Heat.

James did indeed get his first NBA championship with the Heat. He and the "Big 3" then added a second. James decided to go back home for a second stint with the Cavaliers in 2014, and he even led his hometown team to its first NBA championship. But the era of the superteam had begun.

THE PLAYERS' LEAGUE

In the 2015–16 season, the Golden State Warriors won 73 games. That was an NBA record. They had the best three-point shooter of all time in Stephen Curry. Then they added a former Most Valuable Player (MVP).

Kevin Durant signed with the Warriors during the offseason. Echoing the treatment James received, fans criticized Durant for taking the easy way to a championship. But by then, he was hardly alone. In today's NBA, players regularly switch teams in hope of finding the best fit to win a championship.

The NBA promotes its best players to fans. Fans sometimes get upset if they buy tickets to a game and their favorite player is sitting out. One night in 2012, San Antonio Spurs coach Gregg Popovich decided four

Many superteams, such as the Golden State Warriors, have formed in the NBA, leading to criticism that talent isn't evenly distributed across the league.

of his veteran players needed to rest. Instead of suiting up to play Lebron James and the Miami Heat on national television, Tim Duncan, Manu Ginóbili, and two others were sent home.

Popovich was fined $250,000 by the NBA. The league then set rules about how and when players could be rested. It's all a part of the NBA's effort to promote its superstars.

CHAPTER 6

THE WORLD OF
BASKETBALL

Basketball has come a long way since it became an Olympic sport in 1936. The NBA was more than a decade away still. Some of the games were played outdoors. And all the players were amateurs.

The modern Olympic basketball competition is open to professional players—even the biggest stars in the NBA. The growth of basketball at the Olympics was made possible by the 1992 "Dream Team."

That was the nickname given to that year's US Olympic men's basketball team that competed in Barcelona, Spain. The Dream Team easily won the gold medal, defeating its opponents by huge margins. But while the results were great, it was the players on the team that made it special.

caption: The 1992 "Dream Team" celebrates with their gold medals.

That was the first time NBA basketball players were allowed in the Olympics. The United States was able to assemble a team brimming with talent. Several all-time greats including Michael Jordan, Larry Bird, and Magic Johnson were all playing together. The players were treated like celebrities.

The US team was dominant, defeating Cuba by 79 points in its first exhibition game. It beat Angola by 68 points in the tournament opener. Its closest game was a 33-point win against Croatia in the gold-medal game. *Sports Illustrated* later stated that the Dream Team was "arguably the most dominant squad ever assembled in any sport."

SPANNING THE GLOBE

Unless they had access to US television, fans around the world had never seen these superstars play before. Watching this team of future Hall of Famers ignited interest in basketball around the world. It led to the global growth of the sport, making it second only to soccer in popularity.

Talented players from other countries started appearing on NBA rosters. And US Olympic dominance did not last forever. At the Sydney Olympics in 2000, only a last-second miss by Šarūnas Jasikevičius of Lithuania prevented a monumental upset in the semifinals. In Athens, Greece in 2004, the

Americans lost three times, including a 19-point defeat to Puerto Rico in their opener.

The so-called "Redeem Team" featuring Kobe Bryant, LeBron James, and Dwyane Wade won the gold medal against Spain in an epic final at the 2008 Beijing Olympics. Team USA

"Redeem Team" members Michael Redd and Kobe Bryant celebrate after winning the gold medal game in the 2008 Olympics.

was then back on top. The Americans did not lose a game in 2012 and 2016.

However, the Basketball World Cup has been a different story. The US team has had some success, such as winning in 2010 and 2014. But the Americans failed to even reach the semifinals in 2002 and 2019. Those results showed how other countries were rapidly improving as basketball's popularity continues to grow throughout the world.

BASKETBALL IN CHINA

The most popular sports league in China doesn't have a single team located there. It's the NBA, where the league has 150 million followers on social media. More than 300 million people in China play basketball.

NBA games began airing in China in the 1980s. By 1994, Chinese fans could watch live coverage of the NBA Finals. And in 2004, the NBA started playing exhibition games there.

Houston Rockets center Yao Ming, *left*, helped popularize the NBA in China.

Fandom in China became a frenzy when the Houston Rockets drafted Chinese star Yao Ming in 2002. More than 200 million people in China watched his NBA debut. But basketball remained popular in China long after Yao's retirement in 2011. The NBA held its 28th exhibition game there in 2019.

TODAY'S DIVERSE NBA

Basketball may have been an American invention, but players in the NBA today come from all over. Joel Embiid and Pascal Siakam are from Cameroon. Luka Dončić, one of the best young players in the game, is from Slovenia. Giannis Antetokounmpo of the Milwaukee Bucks, the 2019 MVP, is from Greece.

NBA players also come from South America and other parts of Europe and Africa. The rest of the world is quickly catching up to the United States in talent. In August 2019, the United States national team traveled to Australia for some exhibition games. Australia had not beaten the United States in 55 years. The United States had not lost a game since 2006.

But Australia pulled off a historic victory in Melbourne. More than 52,000 fans saw the Boomers beat the Americans 98–94. It gave them hope that their country might contend for a medal at the next Olympic Games.

The Philadelphia 76ers' Joel Embiid is one of the many international basketball players in the NBA.

Basketball started in a gymnasium in Massachusetts in 1891. Dr. James Naismith hung a peach basket on the wall as the first hoop. He drafted 13 original rules. Nearly 120 years later, the game has become one of the most popular sports in the world. From Dr. Naismith's original invention, many innovations came along to help create the modern game of basketball.

TIMELINE

1891

The first game of basketball is played at Springfield College in Massachusetts. The rules were put together by James Naismith.

1936

Basketball becomes an Olympic sport, although professional players aren't allowed to compete for almost 60 years.

1949

The NBA is formed.

1954

Syracuse Nationals owner Danny Biasone proposes use of a 24-second shot clock. It is implemented that fall.

1962

Wilt Chamberlain concludes a historic season in which he averages more than 50 points per game and scored 100 points in a game against the New York Knicks.

1967

The ABA is formed and goes on to last nine seasons, using the three-point shot and adding a slam dunk contest at the All-Star Game.

1979

On October 12, Chris Ford of the Boston Celtics makes the NBA's first three-point shot in a game against the Houston Rockets at Boston Garden.

1984

NBA rookie Michael Jordan signs a $2.5 million shoe contract with Nike to produce Air Jordans.

1992

At the Summer Olympics in Barcelona, the Dream Team thrashes the competition, inspiring a generation of youngsters around the world to begin playing the game.

2016

Stephen Curry of the Golden State Warriors breaks his own record for the third time when he makes 402 three-pointers in a season.

HARLEM GLOBETROTTERS

Basketball promoter Abe Saperstein founded a touring basketball team called the Harlem Globetrotters in 1926. The Globetrotters play exhibition matches that are part basketball game and part entertainment, with players performing exciting dunks and tricks. The Globetrotters play more than 400 live events each year. The players are also known for helping inspire young athletes to play basketball.

SLAM DUNK

Dunks were not a part the early days of basketball. Once players like Julius Erving and Darryl Dawkins made dunks popular in the 1970s, the NBA had a problem. Dunking sometimes bent the hoop and delayed the game. Or worse, in 1979, Dawkins dunked a ball so hard that he broke the rim and shattered the backboard. The NBA started installing hoops that had a hinge and spring so they would not bend as easily.

SYNTHETIC BASKETBALLS

In 2006, the NBA changed the official ball from the standard leather to a new ball made of synthetic materials. Leather balls had to be broken in, were not all the same, and absorbed water. The new ball would fix these issues. But players hated it. It hurt their fingers and was hard to grip. The league switched back after a couple of months. It didn't make another change to the ball until 2020, when it announced Spalding would no longer make NBA basketballs as it had exclusively since 1983.

GLOSSARY

amateurs
People who play a sport without getting paid.

commissioner
The chief executive of a sports league.

expansion
The addition of new teams to increase the size of a league.

field goal
Any basketball shot that isn't a free throw.

folded
Went out of business.

free agent
A player whose rights are not owned by any team.

layup
A shot made from close to the basket; an easy shot.

merged
Joined with another to create something new, such as a company, a team, or a league.

professional
A person who gets paid to do something as a job.

rookie
A professional athlete in his or her first year of competition.

MORE INFORMATION

BOOKS

Ervin, Phil. *Total Basketball*. Minneapolis, MN: Abdo Publishing, 2017.

Felix, Rebecca. *Chuck Taylor: Sneaker Sensation*. Minneapolis, MN: Abdo Publishing, 2018.

Seidel, Jeff. *Ultimate College Basketball Road Trip*. Minneapolis, MN: Abdo Publishing, 2019.

ONLINE RESOURCES

To learn more about innovations in basketball, please visit **abdobooklinks.com** or scan this QR code. These links are routinely monitored and updated to provide the most current information available.

Air Jordan, 28–29
All-Star Game, 16
American Basketball Association (ABA), 15–19
American Basketball League (ABL), 22–23
Antetokounmpo, Giannis, 42

Barry, Rick, 19
Basketball World Cup, 40
Biasone, Danny, 7–9
Bird, Larry, 30, 38
Bosh, Chris, 32
Bryant, Kobe, 22, 39

Chamberlain, Wilt, 20–22
Converse, 26
Curry, Stephen, 24, 34

Dončić, Luka, 42
"Dream Team," 36–38
Duncan, Tim, 35
Durant, Kevin, 34

Embiid, Joel, 42
Erving, Julius "Dr. J.," 16,
expansion, 12–15, 19

four corners offense, 9–11

Gilbert, Dan, 32
Ginóbili, Manu, 35

Harden, James, 34

James, LeBron, 30, 32–35, 39
Johnson, Magic, 30, 38
Jordan, Michael, 28, 38

Kundla, John, 6

McGuire, Frank, 20
Mendenhall, Murray, 6
Mikan, George, 4–6
Ming, Yao, 40–42

Naismith Memorial Basketball Hall of Fame, 28
Naismith, James, 43
National Collegiate Athletic Association (NCAA), 11
Nike, 28

Podoloff, Maurice, 6, 9
Popovich, Gregg, 34–35

"Redeem Team," 39

Saperstein, Abe, 22–23
shot clock, 9–11
Siakam, Pascal, 42
slam dunk contest, 16
Smith, Dean, 9–11
stall tactics, 6–7, 11
superteams, 32–35
Swoopes, Sheryl, 28

Taylor, Chuck, 26–28
Thomas, Isiah, 30
Thompson, Klay, 24–25
three-on-three basketball, 40
three-point shot, 16, 23–25, 34

Wade, Dwayne, 32, 39

ABOUT THE AUTHOR

Chris Sheridan was born in Milwaukee and grew up in New York. Sheridan began covering basketball for the Associated Press in 1992. In addition to the AP, Sheridan founded the basketball site SheridanHoops.com and also worked for ESPN, the *New York Daily News*, and numerous basketball websites. He can still shoot a three-pointer but is much better at layups these days.